# My Liverpool

©2007
Published by The Bluecoat Press, Liverpool
Book design by March Graphic Design Studio, Liverpool
Printed by Grafo

ISBN 1 904438 62 8

**Left** Frank Lenhan in artist Eric Carr's studio.

# My Liverpool

## Photographs by Frank Lenhan

The Bluecoat Press

# Contents

6 Introduction

8 The Royal Daffodil …

9 Mountwood …

10 Ben-my-Chree …

11 Five Isle of Man Steam Packet Company boats …

12 Merchant ship, Eumaeus …

13 Liverpool from Alfred Dock, Birkenhead …

14 The two cathedrals and Albert Dock …

15 West Float, Birkenhead …

16 Snow, Gladstone Dock …

17 Eumaeus leaving port …

18 The nightclub Landfall …

19 Liverpool skyline from Birkenhead …

20 Hold of Texelstroom, Alexandra Dock …

21 Hold of Texelstroom …

22 East Float, Birkenhead …

23 Granary, Gladstone Dock …

24 Lime Street …

25 The main bus terminus at Pier Head …

26 St John's Gardens …

27 St John's Gardens …

28 South Castle Street and Canning Place …

29 South Castle Street …

30 Canning Place …

31 Liverpool Cathedral and Great Georges Street …

32 Early warehouses off Canning Place …

32 Chapel Walk …

33 Litherland Lane / Alley …

33 The Sailors' Home …

34 Metropolitan Cathedral under construction …

35 The Frederic Bowden Memorial Fountain …

36 Bridewell and warehouse, Campbell Street …

37 Palatine public house and the Tobacco Warehouse …

38 The International Hotel, Regent Road …

39 Trafalgar public house …

40 An Everton pub …

41 Myrtle Hotel …

42 Erskine Street and Chapel Street …

43 Gregsons Well …

44 Belgrave Street and Prescot Street …

**45** Prospect Street …

**46** Soho Arms …

**47** Soho Street …

**48** Great Mersey Street …

**49** West Derby Road …

**50** Penton Street …

**51** Empire Street …

**52** Between Brunswick Street and Erskine Street …

**53** Street clearance …

**54** Everton wasteland …

**55** The Church of Christ, Empire Street …

**56** St Benedicts …

**57** St Benedicts …

**58** St Benedicts …

**59** Anfield Weslyan Methodist Church …

**60** Cottenham Street …

**61** Brunswick Street …

**62** The boathouse, Sefton Park …

**63** The pirate ship, Sefton Park …

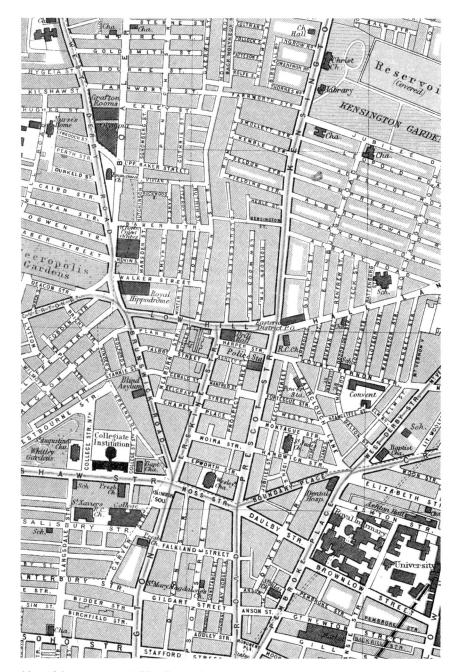

Map of the area around West Derby Road and Erskine Street where Frank Lenhan took many of the photographs in this book.

# Introduction

## by Colin Wilkinson

I first met Frank Lenhan in 1993. Frank had been trying to sell his collection of photographs but, incredibly, had found no interest. The auction houses he visited had advised that they were too recent and would probably attract only a small bid and his approach to local museums and libraries had met with sympathetic ("we would like them as a donation") responses but no hard cash.

Frank was 73 at the time and struggling to make ends meet. He was living on Sheil Road in a rented house and was hoping to move out in the near future. The clutter of a lifetime was being disposed of in anticipation of a new flat and the photographs needed a new home.

We met a couple of times in the following months and I learnt a bit more about his background although, sadly, not enough to write about his life as thoroughly as I now wish. He was Liverpool born, in 1920, and had lived most of his life around Kensington. His father had been a devoutly religious man and deeply involved in the Temperance movement. Some of Frank's earliest memories were of helping to operate the magic lantern at Band of Hope meetings, campaigning against the demon drink.

I have no record of Frank's wartime experiences but, in 1950, he started work as a wharfinger at Gladstone and Toxteth Docks. Frank loved the job and remained in post until 1979. He wrote to me describing his job; "being a wharfinger, the man in charge of receiving and loading all the cargo that was shipped into a vessel. I had to hire and fire all the labour required and I considered it a privilege to work with thousands of dockers, who were a great crowd of men, very generous and amusing and the best dockers in Europe."

Sometime in the early 1960s, Frank bought a camera and started taking photographs. Through his job, he obtained a permit to photograph on the dock estate and his images of the port at that time capture the last years before containerisation changed the industry beyond recognition. Outside of his day job, he started to document the changing city, as whole neighbourhoods were being swept away in a drive to improve the city after wartime bombing and decades of neglect. Terraces after terraces were bulldozed to make way for new estates and old communities broken up and moved out. In the city centre, the historic heart around South Castle Street was ripped out with the loss of some of the earliest surviving merchant houses and warehouses. The fine early Victorian and Georgian facades lining Canning Place were soon to

make way for a failed concrete and glass disaster that lasted less than 30 years before being being turned into landfill. Scandalously, the unique Sailors' Home on Hanover Street was sold off and demolished for a speculative office development that never materialised.

Frank's camera captured the rapidly changing face of Liverpool. The poignant photographs of the woman shutting her door of the last house left standing on the corner of Belgrave Street, children playing outside their condemned house in Prospect Street, the silhouetted ruins of St Benedict's Church in Everton and snow covering the much loved *Jolly Roger* in Sefton Park are images of another Liverpool, lost like the pirate ship in the mists of time.

I bought the photographs off Frank and lost touch with him. He moved out of Shiel Road and, on researching this book, I found out he had died in 2003. Hopefully, this book will be an appropriate farewell to him and to the Liverpool of forty years ago he froze in time so evocatively.

7

The Royal Daffodil returning to Pier Head.

Mountwood crossing to Birkenhead.

Ben-my-Chree, the much-loved Isle of Man Steam Packet Company boat.

A rare sight of five Isle of Man Steam Packet Company boats in dock.

Merchant ship, Eumaeus, sailing down the Mersey with the 'Three Sisters', the chimneys of Clarence Dock power station in the background.

Liverpool from Alfred Dock, Birkenhead, 1974. The Royal Insurance building, nicknamed 'the Sandcastle' is being completed to the left of the Royal Liver Building.

WARNING
LOOK OUT FOR
MEN WORKING
OVER WALL

The two cathedrals and Albert Dock from Morpeth Dock, Birkenhead.

West Float, Birkenhead.

Snow, Gladstone Dock, 1979.

Eumaeus leaving port.

The popular nightclub Landfall berthed in front of the massive Tobacco Warehouse in Stanley Dock. Landfall was an ex-wartime tank landing craft. At the cessation of hostilities it was presented as a gift by a grateful Admiralty, to The Master Mariners of Liverpool who had performed such heroic deeds in the Battles of the Atlantic.

Liverpool skyline from Birkenhead, 1974.

Loading the hold of Texelstroom, Alexandra Dock. In the days before containers, ships were loaded in often dangerous and dirty conditions.

A valuable cargo of Dewars whisky being loaded in to the hold of Texelstroom, Alexandra Dock.

East Float, Birkenhead.

Granary, Gladstone Dock.

24

Lime Street, 1964. The soot and grime covering the buildings gave little idea of the true colour of the stonework.

The main bus terminus at Pier Head 1974.

St John's Gardens, 1965, one of the few green spaces in the city centre.

St John's Gardens 1965. The buildings at the foot of Dale Street were later removed to create a wider exit road from the Queensway Tunnel.

28

The last days of South Castle Street and Canning Place, 1974. The planners had a vision of concrete and glass to replace these fine facades.

South Castle Street, 1974, soon to be demolished to make way for the new Queen Elizabeth Law Courts.

Early warehouses, Canning Place, 1974.

31

Liverpool Cathedral and Great Georges Street, 1974. An area of Georgian houses cleared out and left derelict for years.

Some of Liverpool's earliest warehouses off Canning Place, 1974.

Chapel Walk, 1974. A small pocket of early merchants' houses and warehousing, cleared out in the Derby Square redevelopment.

Litherland Lane / Alley, 1974. Some of the city's earliest warehouses and offices condemned in the name of progress.

The Sailors' Home, 1974. One of the city's most distinguished landmarks, its unnecessary demolition left an ugly, unused plot for 30 years.

Metropolitan Cathedral under construction, 1964.

TAYLOR WOODROW

The Frederic Bowden Memorial
Fountain, West Derby Road, 1975.
Bowden was a leather merchant from
Devon, who arrived in Liverpool as an
18 year old and was deeply involved in
charity work.

Bridewell and warehouse, Campbell Street, 1975. The bridewell is now a restaurant and the warehouse, trendy flats.

Palatine public house and the Tobacco Warehouse, 1975. The Warehouse was the world's largest brick structure at its time of construction.

The International Hotel, Regent Road, 1975. Once pubs like this lined the 'Dock Road'.

Trafalgar public house, Regent Road, 1975.

The impressive tiled facade of an Everton pub, 1975.

Myrtle Hotel, 1976. The days of a pub on every corner were rapidly coming to an end.

Erskine Street and Chapel Street, 1976. The area was being cleared to make way for a business estate.

Gregsons Well, 1973. For years a popular folk club venue.

Last one standing – a house on the corner of Belgrave Street and Prescot Street, 1976. Further down the street is
one of the remaining pre-fabs, emergency post-War housing that hung on until the 1970s.

Prospect Street (between Prescot Street and Erskine Street), 1976.

Soho Arms, corner of Soho Street and Richmond Row, 1976

Soho Street and William Henry Street, 1976.

Fine early nineteenth century housing being demolished on Great Mersey Street, 1976.

West Derby Road, 1975.

49

Penton Street, which ran parallel to Boaler Street and West Derby Road, 1975.

Empire Street, off West Derby Road, 1975.

Between Brunswick Street and Erskine Street, 1973.

Street clearance, between Brunswick Street and Erskine Street, 1973.

Everton wasteland, 1975.

The remains of the Church of Christ, Empire Street, 1975.

Last rites. St Benedicts, 1976.

St Benedicts, 1976.

St Benedicts, 1976.

Anfield Weslyan Methodist Church, Oakfield Road, 1975.

Improvised playground, Cottenham Street, 1973.

Brunswick Street. The chimney of the boiler house of Royal Liverpool Hospital dominates the backgound.

The boathouse, Sefton Park 1979. Vandals set fire to it.

The much-loved pirate ship. Sefton Park, 1979.